COYOTES

by Jennifer Zeiger

Children's Press®

An Imprint of Scholastic Inc.
New York   Toronto   London   Auckland   Sydney
Mexico City   New Delhi   Hong Kong
Danbury, Connecticut

Content Consultant
Dr. Stephen S. Ditchkoff
Professor of Wildlife Sciences
Auburn University
Auburn, Alabama

Photographs © 2014: AP Images/North Wind Picture Archives: 28;
Corbis Images/W. Perry Conway: 5 top, 20; Dreamstime: 1, 46
(Outdoorsman), 2, 3 background, 44, 45 background; Getty Images/
Alex Dissanayake: 32; Media Bakery: 23 (Barbara Magnuson/Larry
Kimball), 4, 5 background, 27 (Chase Swift), 5 bottom, 40; National
Geographic Stock/Alaska Stock Images: 19; Newscom: 36 (David
Stephenson/KRT), 8 (NY Post/Splash News), 12; Photo Researchers:
15 (Art Wolfe/Science Source), 24 (Jeffrey Lepore/Science Source);
Shutterstock, Inc./Ron Hilton: 3, 11; Superstock, Inc.: 7, 39 (Belinda
Images), 31 (imagebroker.net), cover, 35 (Minden Pictures), 16 (NHPA).

Library of Congress Cataloging-in-Publication Data
Zeiger, Jennifer.
  Coyotes / by Jennifer Zeiger.
   p. cm.–(Nature's children)
  Summary: "This book details the life and habits of coyotes."–Provided
by publisher.
  Audience: 9–12.
  Audience: Grades 4 to 6.
  Includes bibliographical references and index.
  ISBN 978-0-531-23356-6 (lib. bdg.) – ISBN 978-0-531-25154-6
(pbk.)
  1. Coyote–Juvenile literature. I. Title. II. Series: Nature's children (New
York, N.Y.)
  QL737.C22Z45 2013
  599.77'25–dc23   2013000092

All rights reserved. Published in 2014 by Children's Press, an imprint
of Scholastic Inc.

Printed in China 62
SCHOLASTIC, CHILDREN'S PRESS, and associated logos are
trademarks and/or registered trademarks of Scholastic Inc.

1 2 3 4 5 6 7 8 9 10 R 23 22 21 20 19 18 17 16 15 14

Coyotes

Class	Mammalia
Order	Carnivora
Family	Canidae
Genus	*Canis*
Species	*Canis latrans*
World distribution	North America, as far north as Alaska and northern Canada; south into Central America; and from the East Coast to the West Coast
Habitats	Originally native to open deserts and grasslands; now also found in temperate forests and tundra, and in both rural and urban areas
Distinctive physical characteristics	Gray or brownish gray backs; whitish neck and belly; reddish fur on legs, ears, and around face; bushy, black-tipped tail; long, narrow snout and pointed ears that stand erect; height of about 24 inches (61 centimeters) at shoulder; length of 3 to 4 feet (0.9 to 1.2 meters) including the tail, which can measure up to 16 inches (40.6 cm)
Habits	Some live in packs that include an alpha male, an alpha female, and their pups; most usually hunt alone or in pairs; territorial, especially during denning season in the spring; mostly nocturnal; highly adaptable and intelligent
Diet	Opportunistic eaters that are largely carnivorous; prefer small mammals, but will also eat deer, amphibians, reptiles, fish, fruits, carrion, and food left out by humans

Contents

CHAPTER 1

Wily Coyotes

A farmer turns off his light, ready to go to sleep at the end of a long day. He hears a long, lonesome-sounding howl rise up from across the prairie. Another joins it, this one from farther away. The farmer wonders if the coyotes will find each other. He also hopes they don't come near his crops.

Hundreds of miles away in a city, a girl hears a garbage can fall in the night. A dog barks nearby. The girl looks out the window and spots an animal that looks like a small German shepherd making a fast getaway. It leaves behind the overturned garbage can, its contents littering the street. The girl wonders if the coyote found any food and hopes the intruder doesn't come back.

Coyotes are renowned for their craftiness. They appear in Saturday morning cartoons and ancient legends. These things are part of what people imagine when they think of coyotes. But what are coyotes really like?

Though coyotes look a lot like dogs, they are wild animals.

All Across the Continent

Coyotes are some of the most adaptive animals on Earth. Because of this, they are found in almost every corner of North America. Coyotes were originally native to the open deserts and grasslands of the central and southwestern United States and northern Mexico. Over the last century, they have spread in all directions and into every nearby habitat, including forests, mountains, and tundra.

By the mid-1900s, they could be found as far north as Alaska and northern Canada, and south into Central America. They thrive in rural and urban areas from the East Coast to the West Coast. Cities such as Chicago, Illinois, and Los Angeles, California, are home to sizable populations of coyotes that are currently being studied by scientists. Strong swimmers, coyotes have even populated islands located close to the mainland, such as the Elizabeth Islands off the coast of Massachusetts.

FUN FACT! The word *coyote* comes from the Aztec word *coyotl*. Coyotes have also been called prairie wolves and brush wolves.

Sometimes coyotes sneak through the streets of large cities in search of food.

Looking at Coyotes

As part of the **canine** family, coyotes look similar to wolves and **domestic** dogs. Observers sometimes confuse them with German shepherds or gray wolves. A coyote's coat is made up of long, coarse hair. Its fur is usually gray or brownish gray along the back and white along the throat and belly. Its legs, ears, and sometimes its face are marked with reddish fur. A coyote's long, bushy tail ends with a black tip. Unlike wolves and dogs, a coyote runs with its tail pointed down. A coyote's eyes are bright yellow, and its snout is long and narrow, opening to reveal a mouth full of sharp teeth.

Coyotes fall between foxes and wolves in size. They weigh between 20 and 50 pounds (9.1 and 22.7 kilograms) and are about 24 inches (61 centimeters) tall from ground to shoulder. Most are between 3 and 4 feet (0.9 and 1.2 meters) long, including their tails. A coyote's tail alone stretches about 16 inches (40.6 cm) in length.

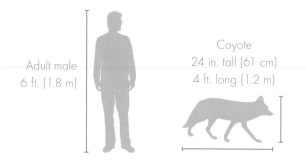

Adult male
6 ft. (1.8 m)

Coyote
24 in. tall (61 cm)
4 ft. long (1.2 m)

A coyote's downward-pointing tail helps set it apart from other canines.

CHAPTER 2

A Master Adapter

Coyotes are experts at surviving. As opportunistic feeders, they will eat almost anything. Usually, coyotes prefer small mammals, such as rabbits and rodents. They also eat larger mammals, such as deer. However, taking down a deer in a hunt is more difficult than catching a rabbit or rat. Coyotes might hunt fish, frogs, snakes, and birds. They've also been known to eat carrion. In late summer and early fall, they eat the plentiful wild fruits and berries.

Around farms and ranches, coyotes might eat sheep, cattle, and other livestock. In urban areas, they sometimes raid garbage cans or pet food that people have left outside. If a feral cat crosses its path, a coyote might eat that, too. Because coyotes are able to eat so many different things, they are capable of living in a wide range of conditions and habitats.

Carrion can provide coyotes with an easy meal when other foods are scarce.

Hunting Season

A variety of natural abilities make coyotes effective hunters. Coyotes have sharp senses of smell and hearing. They also have keen eyesight, even in the dark. They are both good swimmers and fast runners, reaching speeds of about 40 miles (64.4 kilometers) per hour on the ground. Strong jaws and sharp teeth allow them to hold and tear apart their prey.

Depending on their surroundings, coyotes rely on different senses as they hunt. In open areas, such as the prairie or desert, they use their eyesight. They look for the movement of an animal in the prairie grasses or on the empty desert plain. In forests and other areas with dense vegetation that might block their view, coyotes depend more on their hearing and sense of smell.

Coyotes usually hunt alone or in pairs. A single coyote can easily stalk a rodent or other small animal. Coyotes sometimes team up when taking down larger prey. They might take turns chasing a deer until the deer becomes tired and slow.

Small deer make good targets for hungry coyotes.

City Living

Their remarkable ability to adapt has allowed coyotes to thrive even near people. Part of their success in urban areas is connected to the availability of food. People leave food scraps in garbage cans and sometimes keep pet food outdoors, giving coyotes easy access. Large bird feeders attract birds, squirrels, and other seed-eating animals into yards. These animals can then attract coyotes looking for an easy meal.

When looking for cover to sleep, coyotes might hide beneath bridges or inside empty buildings, storm drains, and other human-made structures. Coyotes are experts at hiding. Even when an area is home to several coyotes, people may rarely see them. Coyotes are generally crepuscular, or most active at dawn and dusk. However, they will adjust the timing of their activities if it keeps them from being spotted by a person or other threat.

FUN FACT! Coyotes and badgers sometimes team up. A badger digs prey up from underground into a coyote's reach. A coyote chases prey into a burrow where a badger can catch it.

Easily accessible trash encourages coyotes to approach houses and yards.

CHAPTER 3

Part of the Pack

Some coyotes live as part of a pack. This is especially common for those living in the northeastern United States. Packs generally include between 3 and 10 coyotes. An alpha male and alpha female lead each pack. These two coyotes are called the mating pair. The alphas are the only coyotes in the pack to have young. The other members in the pack are the mating pair's pups. Pups are born each year. Some pups that aren't newly born, but are from previous years' litters, stick around to help raise their new siblings and hunt.

The size of the pack changes depending on the time of year. Packs are often larger during the winter, when food is hardest to find. Hunting together makes the search for food more successful.

Most coyotes, however, do not stick to such rigid social groups. They instead hunt and travel alone or in pairs, forming larger groups only when necessary.

Coyotes sometimes hunt together in small groups,
but most prefer to spend their time alone.

Mating and Denning

Coyotes mate only once a year. This takes place in the winter, usually between January and March. Their litters are born about two months after mating. During pregnancy, the mother looks for a proper **den**. A den requires two things: protection and drainage. Protection can be found in a hollow tree stump or a grouping of rocks covered over by shrubs, trees, or other vegetation. Sometimes a coyote will dig a hole into the ground to create a den. More often, a coyote will steal another animal's den. Woodchucks, raccoons, and skunks all make dens that are suitable for coyotes. Good drainage, usually provided by a slope, keeps the den from being flooded by rain.

Once a pregnant mating pair finds a den, they become fiercely **territorial**. They mark the territory's boundaries with urine and **scat** to warn off other coyotes. They then guard the area to fend off potential threats as they wait for the babies to be born.

Dens help keep pregnant coyotes safe and warm as they prepare to give birth.

A Pup's Life

Coyote litters usually include 4 to 7 pups. But if there is plenty of food available, litters can be as large as 12 pups or more. Some of the largest litters are born in cities.

Like other mammals, coyotes give birth to live young. When pups are born, their eyes are closed and their ears hang limp. They drink their mother's milk. After about 10 days, the pups open their eyes, and their ears stand up. The pups grow stronger, and after two or three weeks, they can venture outside their den. They begin eating regurgitated food from their parents along with the milk. After another few weeks, they begin to take short trips with their parents. They are also weaned and introduced to more solid meat. When they are between four and six months old, they start learning to hunt. After a few months of practice, the pups are able to survive on their own. Males usually leave their parents after six to nine months. Females sometimes stay another year to help raise their mother's next litter.

Pups do not travel far from their den until they grow stronger and more confident.

Facing Threats

Only around a third of all pups survive to adulthood. Few coyotes live more than six years in the wild because they face many threats to their survival. In contrast, captive coyotes may live more than twice as long.

Adult coyotes are a top predator. This means that no other animal hunts them for food. Still, other animals sometimes attack them for different reasons. Wolves often attack coyotes to force them away from good hunting territory and take it for themselves. They have also been known to prey on coyote pups. Pumas sometimes kill coyotes for the same reasons. Humans are another major threat. Sometimes people kill coyotes out of fear or to protect their livestock, crops, pets, or property. Other people kill them for sport or for their coats.

Disease is another issue. Mange is a disease that causes irritated skin and hair loss. In extreme cases, this can result in coyotes freezing during winter or overheating in the summer. Rabies is a dangerous disease that can be transmitted to people and other animals. It eventually kills coyotes that are infected with it.

Coyotes snarl and bare their sharp teeth to warn away threats, which can be another coyote.

Coyote Calls

Coyotes communicate with each other by filling the night air with a variety of calls. One of the easiest to recognize is the howl call. It starts with short yips and ends with a long, high howl. The call can be heard over great distances, and a coyote can tell the identity and the number of coyotes making the sound. Coyotes sometimes call out to tell each other where they are or to warn other coyotes off their territory. A group might make noise when it comes together or when a pup wants to practice the sounds. When a litter is very young, the adults sometimes scatter and call out from different locations. This is to distract possible predators away from the new pups.

Much like domestic dogs, coyotes bark and whine. These sounds might scare away threatening animals or warn other coyotes of danger. A coyote's whine can act as a distress call, informing nearby coyotes that it needs help.

Coyotes tilt their heads back as they howl into the night sky.

CHAPTER 4

Canines Past and Present

Coyotes have been living in North America for a long time. An early coyote ancestor lived in central North America 10 million years ago. This ancient canine was similar in size to a modern-day coyote and likely also hunted small mammals. Over time, the species changed and developed into today's wolves, dogs, and coyotes.

For thousands of years, coyotes were limited to the deserts and prairies of central North America. The animals were well known to local native groups and played an important role as a creator and a trickster in their traditional stories.

During the 20th century, coyotes began to spread across the continent. Most scientists believe this is because the wolf population decreased dramatically during this time. People across the continent began killing wolves out of fear and to protect their property. Without the threat of wolves, coyotes were able to expand their territories.

This ancient cave drawing of a coyote was discovered in New Mexico.

North American Neighbors

Coyotes are part of the **genus** *Canis*, which includes wolves, domestic dogs, jackals, and dingoes. Coyotes' closest relatives are the gray and red wolves and the dogs that share the North American continent.

Like coyotes, wolves are extremely adaptive. They have lived around the world and in almost every type of habitat. Bigger than coyotes, they can weigh as much as 140 pounds (63.5 kg). Their size allows them to take on larger animals, and they are able to chase down prey at speeds up to 40 miles per hour (64.4 kph). They are also known for their nighttime howling, which has uses similar to a coyote's howl.

Many scientists agree that domestic dogs originally came from wolves. People first used wolves as hunting partners and guards thousands of years ago. Over time, these canines were gradually domesticated, and they developed into the different modern-day dog breeds.

Despite their name, gray wolves can be a variety of colors, including white, black, or brown.

Canids on Other Continents

Jackals and dingoes are also part of the *Canis* genus. Jackals are found across Africa and in parts of Europe and Asia. Their food preferences are just as wide as coyotes', if not wider. Though they often hunt small animals and the occasional sheep or antelope, jackals are scavengers, too. They sometimes depend on carrion left by other predators, such as lions.

Scientists debate how exactly dingoes are related to other canids. They know that people introduced dingoes to Australia thousands of years ago. But experts are not sure whether dingoes are feral domestic dogs or if they came directly from wolves. Like wolves, they are exclusively carnivores. They prey on kangaroos, Tasmanian devils, rabbits, and other local mammals. Dingoes are sometimes called singing dogs because of the variety of howl calls they use.

Jackals sometimes come face to face with fearsome lions as they attempt to scavenge carrion.

CHAPTER 5

Adjusting to New Neighbors

Many North American carnivores are disappearing. But this is far from true for coyotes. Scientists estimate that there are more coyotes now than ever before. This is in spite of hunting, poisoning, trapping, and other human efforts to decrease the coyote population.

These cunning creatures are being spotted more often and in more locations across the continent all the time. Many coyotes have claimed city parks as part of their territories. Others live in and around golf courses. Golf greens are mowed and kept open, much like the open spaces of the coyote's original desert and prairie habitats. Coyotes living by fire stations have been heard howling along with the sirens of emergency vehicles. They have even been spotted at night, patrolling their territory down major city streets such as Michigan Avenue in Chicago, Illinois.

The steady increase in coyote numbers has worried many people. What problems might these animals cause? How can people prevent these problems?

Coyotes are often hit by cars as they try to cross busy streets.

Problems

Coyotes have always caused problems for ranchers and farmers. They might prey on livestock, such as cattle, sheep, goats, or pigs. Coyotes may eat fruit and vegetable crops. Attacks on both livestock and crops cost farmers and ranchers money. Coyotes have also been known to attack dogs and cats. Usually the coyote prey are feral animals that do not belong to anyone, but sometimes they are people's pets. The coyote might kill a dog or cat for food. More often, however, the coyote attacks to protect its territory. Some people are afraid that coyotes will attack people. This is extremely rare, though. It usually happens because the coyote is sick.

Coyote diseases can create problems for people. Rabies, mange, and other diseases can be passed to other animals, especially dogs. This threatens the health of people, their pets, and their livestock.

Farmers install fences to help prevent coyotes from attacking livestock.

Benefits

Coyotes are not all bad for humans. There can be great benefits to having coyotes living in or near your area. The most important benefit is that coyotes are what researchers call a biocontrol. This means they help keep the populations of other animals under control.

For example, deer populations can sometimes grow too big. Large numbers of deer can change a forest's structure. This can affect life for other species living in the forest. Coyotes are a major predator of fawns, or young deer. Preying on fawns helps keep the deer population from growing too quickly. Coyotes also prey on goose eggs, so they serve the same purpose with goose populations.

Rats and other rodents can spread disease. Coyotes help keep rodent populations down, especially in urban areas. Studies have found that when the coyote population decreases in an area, the local rodent population increases dramatically.

Rodents have been known to spread dozens of different diseases to humans.

Finding a Balance

Researchers are still studying the effects of coyotes in urban and rural areas. They are also looking at how coyotes manage to survive in spite of human actions. The more they learn, the better people will understand what it means to have coyote neighbors.

The best thing most people can do is to discourage coyotes from visiting their homes. Coyotes are naturally afraid of humans. However, it is still a good idea to avoid doing things that will attract them. What can you do? If possible, put trash outside only when it is time for it to be picked up by the garbage collectors. Never keep pet food outside. If you see a coyote, scare it away by waving your arms and making loud noises. Bang on a pot if you have one handy. Never run away. And if a coyote returns or doesn't seem afraid, tell an adult. Call the police or your local wildlife department.

Coyotes are master survivors. If everyone works together, people will find a way to live safely and comfortably with these canines.

Scientists use radio collars to track coyotes' movements in the wild.

Words to Know

adaptive (uh-DAP-tiv) — able to make something work in a different way or for a different purpose

alpha (AL-fuh) — socially dominant, especially in a group of animals

canine (KAY-nine) — of or having to do with dogs

captive (KAP-tiv) — held or trapped by people

carrion (KAR-ee-uhn) — dead and putrefying flesh

crepuscular (kre-PUS-kyuh-lur) — most active at dusk and dawn

den (DEN) — the home of a wild animal

domestic (duh-MES-tik) — animals that have been tamed; people use them as a source of food or as work animals, or keep them as pets

feral (FEH-rul) — wild, having escaped from domestication

genus (JEE-nuhs) — a group of related plants or animals that is larger than a species but smaller than a family

mammals (MAM-uhlz) — warm-blooded animals that have hair or fur and usually give birth to live babies

mating (MAYT-ing) — joining together to produce babies

opportunistic (ah-pur-too-NIS-tik) — taking advantage of opportunities as they arise

predator (PRED-uh-tur) — an animal that lives by hunting other animals for food

prey (PRAY) — an animal that is hunted by another animal for food

rabies (RAY-beez) — a viral disease of the nervous system of mammals that is usually transmitted by the bite of a rabid animal; characterized by abnormal behavior, paralysis, and eventually death if untreated

regurgitated (ri-GUR-juh-tate-id) — food that has been swallowed and brought back up to the mouth

rural (RUR-uhl) — having to do with the countryside, country life, or farming

scat (SKAT)—feces

scavengers (SKAV-uhn-jurz) — people or animals that search through garbage for something useful or edible

species (SPEE-sheez) — one of the groups into which animals and plants of the same genus are divided; members of the same species can mate and have offspring

stalk (STAWK) — to hunt or track an animal in a quiet, secret way

territorial (terr-uh-TOR-ee-uhl) — defensive of a certain area

tundra (TUHN-druh) — a very cold area of northern Europe, Asia, and Canada where there are no trees and the soil under the surface of the ground is always frozen

urban (UR-buhn) — having to do with or living in the city

vegetation (vej-uh-TAY-shuhn) — plant life or the plants that cover an area

weaned (WEEND) — gradually stopped the reliance on mother's milk for nourishment

Habitat Map

NORTH AMERICA

SOUTH AMERICA

PACIFIC OCEAN

ATLANTIC

Coyote Range

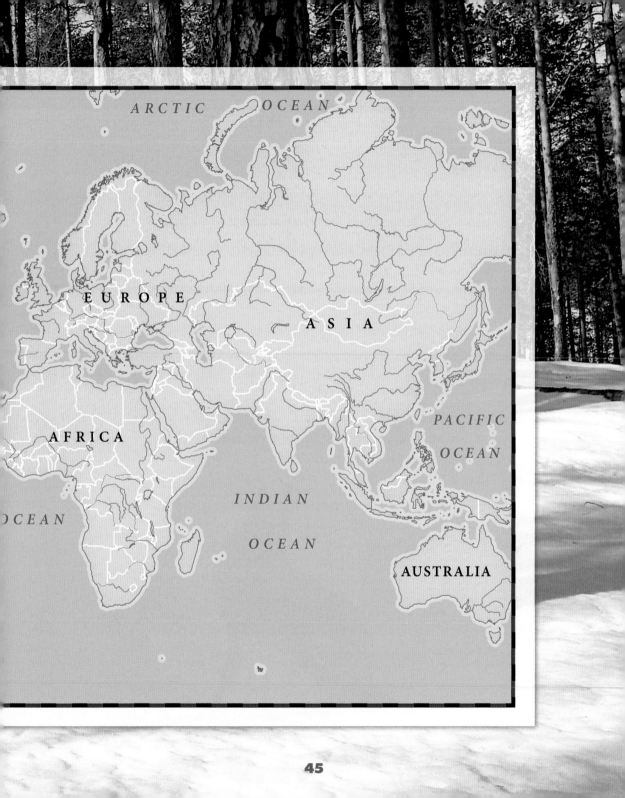

ARCTIC OCEAN

EUROPE

ASIA

AFRICA

PACIFIC OCEAN

OCEAN

INDIAN

OCEAN

AUSTRALIA

45

Find Out More

Books

Read, Tracy C. *Exploring the World of Coyotes*. Buffalo, NY: Firefly Books, 2011.

Roza, Greg. *Your Neighbor the Coyote*. New York: Windmill Books, 2012.

Vogel, Julia, and Andrew Recher. *Coyotes*. Minnetonka, MN: NorthWord Books for Young Readers, 2007.

Visit this Scholastic Web site for more information on coyotes:
www.factsfornow.scholastic.com
Enter the keyword **Coyotes**

Index

Page numbers in *italics* indicate a photograph or map.

About the Author

Jennifer Zeiger lives in Chicago, Illinois, where she writes and edits children's nonfiction books. She remembers hearing coyotes howling at night while growing up in a small town in Missouri.